Reading Age 5-6

Brad Thompson

In a strange place, not too far from here, lives a scare of monsters.

A 'scare' is what some people call a group of monsters, but these monsters are really very friendly once you get to know them.

They are a curious bunch – they look very unusual, but they are quite like you and me, and they love learning new things and having fun.

In this book you will go on a learning journey with the monsters and are sure to have lots of fun along the way.

Visit our website to meet the monsters and upload your drawings to the Monster Gallery.

Contents

2 Monster Text Types
4 A Monster Story
6 Monster Letters
8 Monster Fact Finding
10 Monster Meanings
12 Incredible Instructions
14 Monster Challenge 1
16 Who Said That?
18 Riddles about Monsters
20 What's Happening?
22 Dictionary Time
24 A Monster Advert
26 Whatever Next?
28 Monster Challenge 2
30 Answers
32 Monster Match

Monster Text Types

Kora is sorting out some monster books.
There are lots of different types of books.
She has got into a monster muddle!
She needs to know which type of book
is which.
She has some labels to help her remember.
Kora matches one up.

have a start, middle and end → Stories

1 Draw lines to match the books to the correct label card.

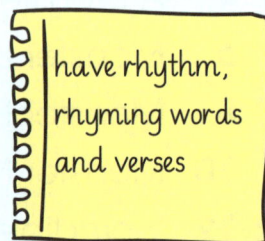

Instructions

Poems

Stories

have characters and a start, a middle and an end

have numbered steps and a list of what you need

have rhythm, rhyming words and verses

2 Kora has a set of instructions to build a monster den.

Write the headings from the box below in the correct place in the instructions.

How to make a monster den	What to do	You will need

```
[                                    ]

[                                    ]
```

- a big cloth
- three big sticks
- rope

```
[                                    ]
```

1. Stand the three sticks up together.
2. Wrap the cloth around them.
3. Use rope to tie the cloth to the sticks.

Fun Zone!

Make a monster pencil pot!

Well done! You can now find and colour **Shape 1** on the Monster Match page!

Monster Pencil Pot

You will need a juice carton, PVA glue, newspaper, paint, felt tips and scissors.

Ask an adult to help when needed.

1 Wash the carton out.
2 Carefully cut the top off the carton.
3 Coat the carton in PVA glue.
4 Cover the carton in lots of small bits of newspaper.
5 Cover the newspaper in glue.
6 Leave to dry.
7 Use your felt tips and/or paint to decorate your pencil pot in a monster way.

A Monster Story

Poggo has written Mum a story.
It is about what happened to some of
his monster friends.
Poggo has split the story into three parts.

Read each part of the story.
Then answer the questions.
Write in full sentences for Questions 2 and 3.

1

Kora was on her way to the shop to buy some monster juice because there was none left at home. When she got there, the shop was shut. Just then, Fizz arrived.
"Hello Kora," said Fizz.
Fizz could tell that Kora was not happy.
"What is wrong?" asked Fizz.
"The shop is shut and I can't buy any monster juice," replied Kora.

Tick ✓ the box next to the correct answer.

a Why did Kora go to the shop?

There was no juice at home. ☑   She had run out of jam. ☐

b Why was Kora unhappy?

The shop was shut. ☑   She hurt her leg. ☐

2

"Don't be sad – come to my house and I will give you a carton of juice," said Fizz. When they arrived at Fizz's house, Fizz gave Kora some juice to take home.
"Thank you," said Kora. She went home feeling much happier.

a Where did Kora and Fizz go to get some juice?

Fizz hase

b How did Kora feel when she got the juice?

hapy

3

"Mum, I have the monster juice!" shouted Kora.
"Don't worry, I bought a carton on my way home," replied Mum.
"Well, at least we have two cartons now," said Kora. She drank the monster juice with a smile on her face.

a How many cartons of monster juice did Kora and her Mum have now?

2

b Why do you think Kora had a smile on her face?

cos she hap tow

Fun Zone!

It is time to write a monster story!

Continue this monster story on a separate piece of paper.

That is a great story! You can now find and colour **Shape 2** on the Monster Match page!

I will never forget the day I met the purple monster…

What will happen next? How will it end?

Monster Letters

Litmus is writing a letter to the Professor.
He is saying thank you for helping him with his monster experiments.

He has almost finished the letter but he is unsure of the meaning of some of the words.

1 Help Litmus complete his letter to the Professor.

Read the letter on the next page.
Write the words from the container below in the correct gaps.
Think about what each word means before you choose it.

sure

wait

thank

grow

discovery

good

thrilled

Dear Professor,

I want to _____ you for your help with my monster experiments.

The results have been very _____.

I now know that monsters _____ best when they have lots

of sleep and monster juice.

The monsters will love my _____.

I am _____ that they will be _____.

I cannot _____ to come to science class at Monsterville school!

Best wishes,

Litmus

Fun Zone!

Make your own balloon rocket!

Rocketastic! You can now find and colour **Shape 3** on the Monster Match page!

Balloon Rocket

You will need a balloon, one long piece of string (about 2m), a plastic straw and sticky tape.

Ask an adult to help when needed.

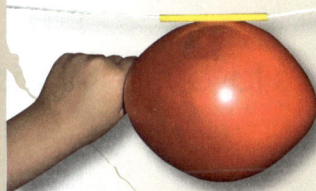

1 Tie one end of the string to a chair.

2 Push the other end of the string through the straw.

3 Pull the string tight and tie it to another chair.

4 Blow up the balloon (but don't tie it).

5 Pinch the end of the balloon and tape the balloon to the straw.

6 Let go and watch the balloon rocket fly!

Monster Fact Finding

Gran and I love learning interesting facts.
We know lots of things about the monsters.

I have written fact files about two of the monsters – Webber and Tizz.

1 Look at the picture of Webber and read his fact file.
Tick ✓ the box next to the correct answer.

Description: Webber has lots of eyes and arms.
This means he is great at doing lots of things at once.
He is very tidy.
He likes telling the time.
Favourite things: His pocket watch and hat.

a What does Webber like doing?

Telling the time ☐

Fixing cars ☐

b What are Webber's favourite things?

Nuts and bolts ☐

His pocket watch and hat ☐

2   Look at the picture of Tizz and read her fact file.
Answer the questions in full sentences.

Description: Tizz has a sister called Fizz. They are twins.
This means that they were born at around the same time.
They may be twins but they are very different.
Tizz was born first. Tizz calls Fizz 'little sister'.
Favourite things: Her camera, making scrapbooks and
having sleepovers with Fizz and Kora.
Pet hate: Boggle-eyed mini-monsters.

a   Who was born first, Tizz or Fizz?

_____

b   What does Tizz like to do with Fizz and Kora?

_____

c   What does Tizz hate?

_____

Fun Zone!

Draw your own monster.

Think about: hair/fur colour,
arms, legs, eyes and clothes.

Brilliant! You can now find
and colour **Shape 4** on the
Monster Match page!

Monster Meanings

Dad has been helping me with lots of different words.

He says that some words are spelt and sound the same.

These words are called **homonyms**. We have to be really careful that we use the correct meaning of words.

For example, Dad says that the word 'club' can mean:

- a club that someone can join, like a book **club**
- a golf **club** that a golfer uses to hit the ball.

1 Help Kora choose the correct meanings for the homonym 'squash' by ticking ✓ two of the three boxes.

☐ A drink made with water

☐ A type of musical instrument

☐ When you crush something

2 Help Kora choose one word to fill the gap in both sentences.

a

set	match	game

Fizz wants to go to the basketball _____.

Fizz only wears socks that _____.

b

jar	bank	purse

Mum needs to put some monster money in the _____.

Mum loves to sit and read by the river _____.

3 Help Kora match the homonyms by drawing lines between the pictures and the correct word.

orange

band

cricket

Fun Zone!

Have fun with hand printing!

Fantastic! You can now find and colour **Shape 5** on the Monster Match page!

Hand Printing Wrapping Paper

You will need coloured paint, paintbrushes and paper.

Ask an adult to help when needed.

1 Paint your hand any colour you want.
2 Press it onto the paper.
3 Turn the paper so that the hand print is facing a different direction.
4 Find a new space on the paper and again, press your hand onto the paper.
5 Repeat steps 1–4 until the paper is covered.

Incredible Instructions

Tizz is very happy.
She has bought a new camera.

There are instructions for how
to use the camera.
Tizz needs your help to follow the
instructions, so she can start
using her camera.

Here are the instructions for Tizz's camera.
Read the instructions, then answer the
questions on the next page.

Instructions
1. Take the camera out of the box.
2. Put the batteries in the camera.
3. Point the camera.
4. Press the red button to take a picture.

1 Read each sentence.
Tick ✓ the box next to the correct answer.

a What is the first thing that Tizz needs to do?

Take the camera out of the box. ☐

Put the batteries in the camera. ☐

b What does Tizz need to do after she has put the batteries in the camera?

Take the camera out of the box. ☐

Point the camera. ☐

c What is the final thing Tizz needs to do?

Press the red button to take a picture. ☐

Take the camera out of the box. ☐

Fun Zone!

Design your own monster scrapbook!

Congratulations! You can now find and colour **Shape 6** on the Monster Match page!

Monster Scrapbook

You will need five sheets of A4 paper or card, a hole punch, string, scissors, and pencils, crayons or felt tips.

Ask an adult to help when needed.

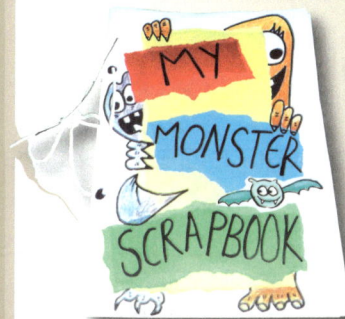

1 Fold each sheet of paper or card in half.

2 Put the folded sheets inside each other to make a booklet.

3 Punch holes in the middle of the paper at the edge where it is folded.

4 Thread one piece of string through the hole at the bottom and one through the hole at the top.

5 Tie a knot for each one.

6 Colour in the front cover.

7 Fill the book with your favourite monster photos or pictures.

Monster Challenge 1

1 Read the information and then answer the questions.
Tick ✓ the box next to the correct answer.

> There are eight types of monsters in the monster world. They all look very different. There are even monster pets. So far, only two different types have been discovered.

a How many types of monsters are there?

Eight ☐   Ten ☐

b How many types of monster pets have been discovered?

Three ☐   Two ☐

2 Read the information about Otto and then answer the questions.

> This is Otto. He is a monster that is just a brain.
> He needs a robot suit to do what he wants to do.
> This **kind** of monster controls their suit with brain power!

a Choose the correct meanings for the homonym '**kind**' by ticking two of the three boxes.

☐ A type of hat

☐ When someone is nice to someone else

☐ Types of animals or other things

b How does Otto control his suit?
Answer in a full sentence.

_____

3 Read the information about the monsters.

Choose the correct words from the box to fill in the gaps.
Think about what each word means before you choose it.

eyes	telling	measured	facts	good

Webber has lots of _____ and lots of arms.

This means he is _____ at doing lots of jobs

at the same time.

He likes measuring things and _____ the time.

Webber could tell you lots of _____ about

the things he has _____!

4 Read the information about Kora.
Then answer the questions in full sentences.

Kora can breathe on land and under water.
She has webbed feet, which means she is very good
at swimming.
She is very quiet and shy when you first meet her.
Once you get to know her she is great fun.

a What is Kora good at?

_____

_____

b What is Kora like when you first meet her?

_____

_____

Who Said That?

I am reading books with Gran.
We are looking at speech bubbles.
Gran says that if there are speech bubbles, you need to look at the whole picture.
This is so you can see what is happening in the story.

"Oh no! My ball!"

"It's too dangerous to get!"

1 Look at the picture.
Write in the speech bubbles what you think Mum and Dad are saying to each other.

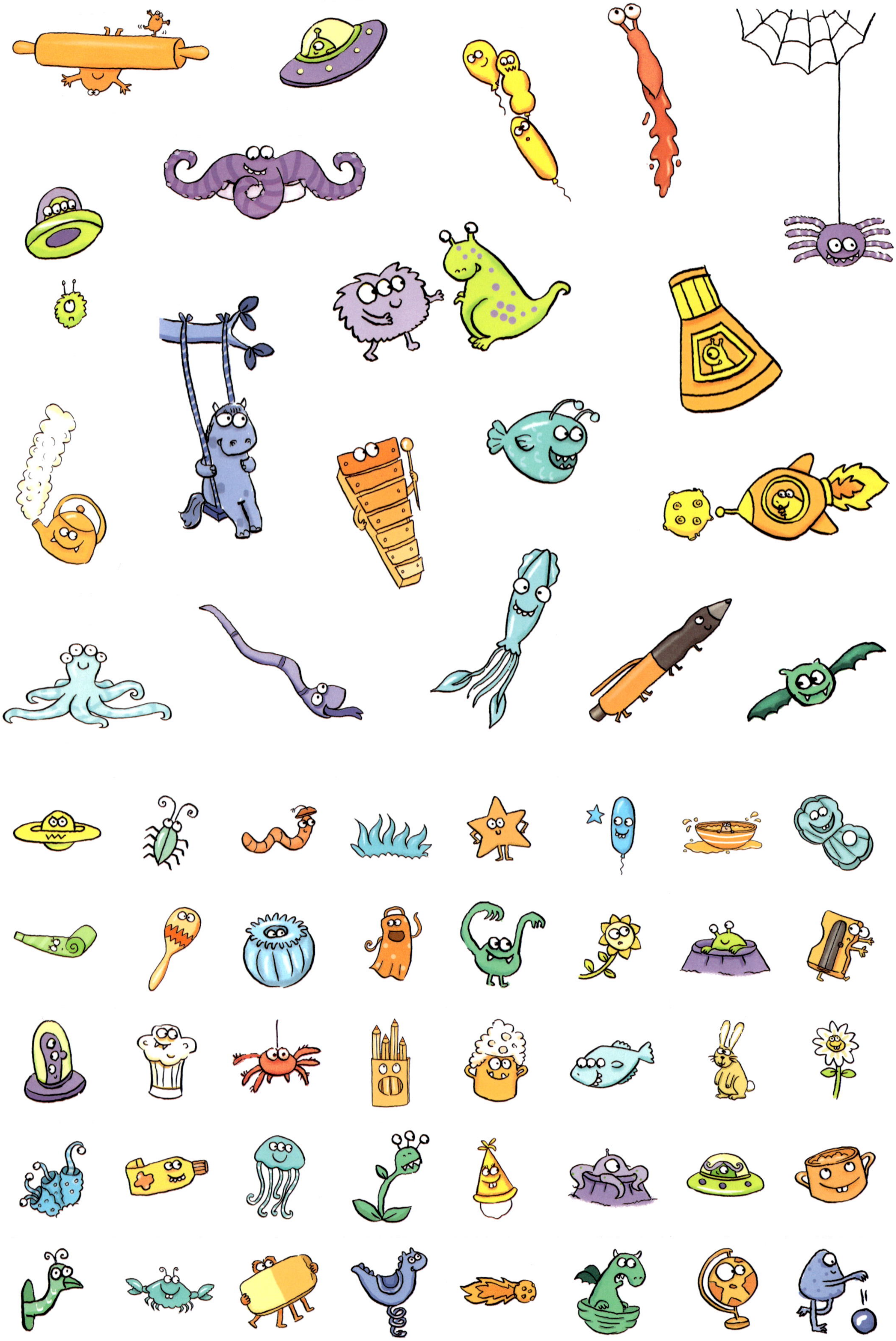

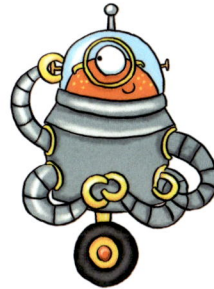

2 Look at the pictures.

a Write in the speech bubble what you think the Professor is saying to Litmus.

"Will monster juice mix with monster shampoo?"

_____

_____

b Write in the speech bubble what you think Gran is saying to Tizz.

"I hope we see some bugs!"

_____

_____

Fun Zone!

Let's make some monster mouths!

Fantabulous! You can now find and colour **Shape 7** on the Monster Match page!

Monster Mouths!

You will need a sheet of A4 paper or card, four lollipop sticks, glue or sticky tape, scissors, and pencils, crayons or felt tips.

Ask an adult to help when needed.

1 Fold the sheet of card in half and half again.

2 Cut along the fold so you have four pieces of card the same size.

3 Design a monster mouth on each piece of card – fill the space as much as you can.

4 Think about colour, and the monsters' teeth, lips and tongues.

5 Cut the mouths out and stick a lollipop stick to the back of each one.

Riddles about Monsters

Poggo is learning about **riddles**.
A riddle is a type of poem.
You have to use clues to work out
what something or someone is.

The first clue could have
many answers.
The last clue usually helps
to give the answer!

Here is a riddle:

> I am a monster.
> I am blue.
> I like skateboarding.
>
> **That's right, I am Poggo!**

1 Use the pictures and the clues to work out
who the riddles on the next page are describing.
Write your answers on the lines.

Litmus

The Professor

Tizz

Fizz

Zak

Leckie

a

I am green.
I wear a white coat.
I have a red cap.

_____

b

I have a tail.
I am purple.
I play basketball.

_____

c

I do not wear a hat.
I am a pet.
I am green with yellow spots.

_____

Fun Zone!

Create a riddle about yourself!

Monsterific! You can now find and colour **Shape 8** on the Monster Match page!

Ridiculous Riddles

Think of three clues about yourself. Write them on the lines.

Remember, the first clue could describe many people. The last clue shows that it is you!

_____

_____

_____

What's Happening?

I am reading a monster picture book with Rif. The pictures in the stories are like clues. They help tell us what is happening in the story.

1 Look at the picture and text.

Answer the questions on the next page in full sentences.

Dad asks Rif, "How many robot arms does Otto have?"
Rif says, "Otto has four robot arms."

a What colour is Poggo's skateboard?

_____

_____

b How many monsters are cheering on Poggo and Otto?

_____

_____

c What are Poggo and Otto doing?

_____

_____

d Why is Poggo's hat in the air?

_____

_____

e Why does Otto have a happy face?

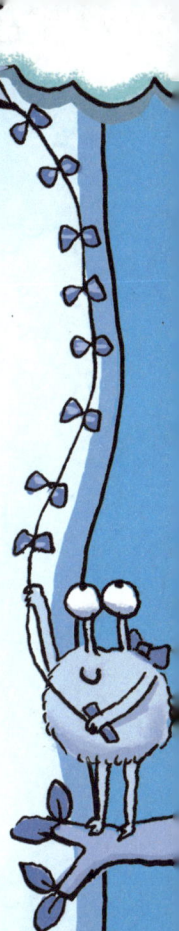

_____

_____

Fun Zone!

Join the dots to complete the picture of the monster. Colour it in. Who is it?

Fantastic! You can now find and colour **Shape 9** on the Monster Match page!

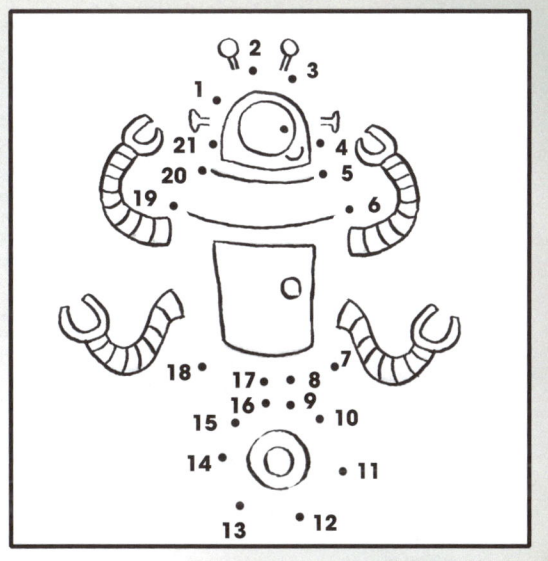

Dictionary Time

I am teaching the little monsters, Rif, Dot and Noo, how to use a **dictionary**.
A dictionary tells us the meaning of words.
It is written in alphabetical order, from **a** to **z**.

1 Here is a page from a dictionary.

beside - bitter

beside PREPOSITION
If something is **beside** something else, it is at the side of it.

best ADJECTIVE
Best means the "most good", or better than anything else. *That's the **best** programme I've seen.*

better
ADJECTIVE **1** Something that is **better** than something else is of a higher standard or quality. *Your bicycle is **better** than mine.*
ADJECTIVE **2** **Better** can also mean more sensible. *It would be **better** to go home.*
ADJECTIVE **3** If you are feeling **better** after an illness, you are not feeling so ill.

between PREPOSITION
If something is **between** two other things, it is in the space or time that separates them. *The toyshop is **between** the bank and the library.*

beware VERB
You tell people to **beware** if there is danger of some kind. ***Beware** of the bull.*

Bible **Bibles** NOUN
The **Bible** is the sacred book of the Christian religion.

bicycle **bicycles** NOUN
A **bicycle** is a vehicle with two wheels. You sit on it and turn pedals with your feet to make it go.

big **bigger, biggest** ADJECTIVE
Something or somebody **big** is large in size or importance.

bike **bikes** NOUN
Bike is an abbreviation of **bicycle**.

bill **bills**
NOUN **1** A **bill** is a piece of paper saying how much money you owe. *Mum's just had the electricity **bill**.*
NOUN **2** A bird's **bill** is its beak.

bin **bins** NOUN
A **bin** is a container, usually with a lid, for putting rubbish in.

bind **binds, binding, bound** VERB
If you **bind** something, you tie something like string or cloth tightly round it so that it is held in place.

biology NOUN
Biology is the study of living things.

bird **birds** NOUN
A **bird** is an animal with two legs, two wings and feathers.

birth **births** NOUN
The **birth** of a baby is when it comes out of its mother's body.

birthday **birthdays** NOUN
Your **birthday** is a special date that is remembered every year, because it was the day you were born.

biscuit **biscuits** NOUN
A **biscuit** is a small, flat, crisp kind of cake.
See Other foods on page 261

bit **bits**
NOUN **1** A **bit** of something is a small piece of it.
NOUN **2** A **bit** is a piece of metal that goes in a horse's mouth.
VERB **3** **Bit** is also the past tense of **bite**.

bite **bites, biting, bit, bitten** VERB
If you **bite** something, you use your teeth to hold, cut or tear it.

bitter
ADJECTIVE **1** If something has a **bitter** taste, it tastes sharp and unpleasant.
ADJECTIVE **2** Someone who is **bitter** feels angry and disappointed.

a
b
c
d
e
f
g
h
i
j
k
l
m
n
o
p
q
r
s
t
u
v
w
x
y
z

23

Use the dictionary page to help you complete each sentence.

a **Biology** is the study of _____ .

b A **bicycle** is a _____ .

c Someone who is **bitter** feels _____

_____ .

2 Answer the questions below about the dictionary page.

a What is the page number? _____

b Why do you think the page includes pictures?

_____

_____

c Why is the alphabet written down the side of the page?

_____

_____

Fun Zone!

Use a child's dictionary to answer these questions. Write your answers on a separate piece of paper. Ask an adult to help when needed.

Brilliant work! You can now find and colour **Shape 10** on the Monster Match page!

1 Write the name of the dictionary.

2 What is the first word listed in the dictionary?

3 What is the last word listed in the dictionary?

4 How many pages does the dictionary have?

5 How many pages of words starting with **x** are there in the dictionary?

A Monster Advert

Poggo is selling his skateboard. He writes an advert to tell the other monsters how much fun it is to use.

1 Look at the advert and answer the questions that follow.

FOR SALE

Super skateboard
Very good condition
Four new wheels

You will go very fast!
You will do amazing tricks!
You will be the coolest monster!

See Poggo to find out more.

Tick ✓ the box if the sentence is true.
Cross ✗ the box if the sentence is false.

a Poggo's skateboard is green. ☐

b Poggo's skateboard has four new wheels. ☐

c See Tizz for more information about the skateboard. ☐

d You will not be able to do amazing tricks. ☐

e You will be the coolest monster. ☐

f You will go very slowly. ☐

Fun Zone!

Let's make some monster feet.

Stomplastic! You can now find and colour **Shape 11** on the Monster Match page!

Monster Feet

You will need two empty rectangular tissue boxes, sticky tape, paint, card, newspaper and PVA glue.

Ask an adult to help when needed.

1 Cut away any plastic around the opening on top of the tissue boxes.

2 Cut six triangular 'claws' from the card.

3 Use glue to stick three pieces of card to the front of each tissue box. Let the glue dry completely.

4 Cover the boxes and claws with PVA glue and newspaper. Leave to dry.

5 Paint the boxes and claws.

6 Use pieces of scrunched-up newspaper to make the boxes fit your feet.

7 Stomp away!

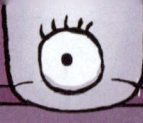

Whatever Next?

Webber is very good at making **predictions**.
A prediction is what you think is going to happen next.
When you make a prediction, you need to use clues from the text or a picture.

For example, Webber sees Kora and predicts that she will drop her books because she is carrying too many of them.

1 Look at the pictures and predict what will happen next.

a

_____

_____

b

_____

_____

Read the text and predict what will happen next.

a

Fizz was in the garden playing basketball with a friend. One of her shoelaces was undone.

_____

_____

b

Tizz went to the park – it was very sunny so she did not take her coat. When she got to the park there were grey clouds. She started taking photos. Suddenly, she felt a drop of water on her nose.

_____

_____

Fun Zone!

Find five differences between these two pictures of Webber.

Very good! You can now find and colour **Shape 12** on the Monster Match page!

Monster Challenge 2

Below is a newspaper report.

Read it carefully.

Then answer the questions on the following page in full sentences.

25th May

Monster News

Litmus Wins Science Award!

On Monday, Litmus won the award for the Young Monster Scientist of the Year. Otto, the Professor, Webber, Mum and Dad were all there.

Litmus won the award for his monster growth experiment.

"I found that if little monsters have lots of sleep and monster juice, they grow much bigger, and become very loud and scary," said Litmus.

Monsters are now starting to sleep lots and drink as much monster juice as they can. They all want to be the scariest monster around.

It was no surprise to many monsters that Litmus won the award.

His mum said, "Litmus has always loved science. I am really proud of him!"

Litmus said, "I can't believe I have won. I never thought I would! I am so happy."

1 Which monster has won an award?

_____

2 On which day of the week did he win the award?

_____

3 Name two monsters who went to the awards.

1 _____

2 _____

4 What makes the little monsters grow and become loud and scary?
Tick ✔ the boxes next to the correct answers.

Lots of sleep ☐

Monster snacks ☐

Monster juice ☐

5 How did Litmus' mum feel when Litmus won the award?

_____

_____

6 How did Litmus feel about winning the award?

_____

_____

I knew you could do it!
You have made it to the end of the book.
You are a magnificent monster!

Answers

Page 2

1

Page 3

2

How to make a monster den

You will need

- a big cloth
- three big sticks
- rope

What to do

1. Stand the three sticks up together.
2. Wrap the cloth around them.
3. Use rope to tie the cloth to the sticks.

Page 4

1 a There was no juice at home. ☑

b The shop was shut. ☑

Page 5

2 a They went to Fizz's house.

b Kora felt much happier.

3 a Kora and her mum had two cartons.

b She could finally drink the juice.

Page 7

1 Child to write the words in this order:
thank; good; grow; discovery; sure;
thrilled; wait

Page 8

1 a Telling the time ☑

b His pocket watch and hat ☑

Page 9

2 a Tizz was born first.

b Tizz likes to have sleepovers with
them.

c Tizz hates boggle-eyed mini-monsters.

Page 10

1 ☑ A drink made with water

☑ When you crush something

Page 11

2 a match **b** bank

3

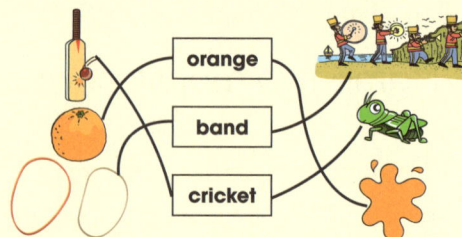

Page 13

1 a Take the camera out of the box. ☑

b Point the camera. ☑

c Press the red button to take a
picture. ☑

Page 14

1 a Eight ☑

b Two ☑

2 a When someone is nice to
someone else ☑

Types of animals or other things ☑

b He controls his suit with brain power.

Page 15

3 Child to write the words in this order:
eyes, good, telling, facts, measured

4 a Kora is very good at swimming.

b She is very quiet and shy when you
first meet her.

Page 16

1 Child to write appropriate speech, for
example: "Wow! What a view!" and
"I wonder what that is?"

Page 17

2 a Child to write appropriate speech, for
example: "We will soon find out!"

b Child to write appropriate speech, for
example: "Me too, I love exploring!"

Page 19
1 **a** Litmus   **b** Fizz   **c** Zak

Page 21
1 **a** Poggo's skateboard is red.
 b Five monsters are cheering on Poggo and Otto.
 c Poggo and Otto are having a race.
 d Poggo's hat has blown off because he is moving so fast.
 e Otto has a happy face because he is about to win the race.

Fun Zone!

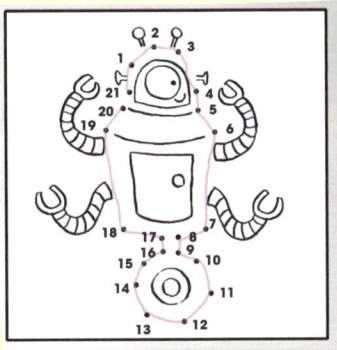

Page 23
1 **a** Biology is the study of living things.
 b A bicycle is a vehicle with two wheels.
 c Someone who is bitter feels angry and disappointed.
2 **a** 23
 b They make the page colourful; they help you understand words.
 c The letters are like signposts; on this page the b is highlighted so you know the words start with b.

Fun Zone!
Child to answer questions with reference to their own dictionary.

Page 25
1 **a** ✗   **b** ✓   **c** ✗   **d** ✗   **e** ✓   **f** ✗

Page 26
1 Child to write appropriate predictions, for example:
 a Nano crawls to the bottle and drinks the milk.
 b Otto builds something.

Page 27
2 Child to write appropriate predictions, for example:
 a Fizz falls over because she trips over her shoelace.
 b Tizz gets wet because she hasn't brought her coat.

Fun Zone!

Page 29
1 Litmus has won an award.
2 He won the award on Monday.
3 Two monsters who went to the awards were the Professor and Otto. (Also accept: Webber, Mum, Dad.)
4 Lots of sleep   ☑
 Monster juice   ☑
5 Litmus' mum felt very proud.
6 Litmus felt very happy. He could not believe he had won.

Monster Match

Each time you complete a topic in this book, you will be awarded a shape number.

Find and colour the shapes in the picture of the Professor that match the numbers you have been given.

As you work through the book you will gradually see the Professor come to life!